Who Was Frank Sinatra?

by Ellen Labrecque

illustrated by Manuel Gutierrez

Penguin Workshop

To Lynn Muckerman and all my best
Hoboken girls—I hope we brunch forever—EL

To my brother Francisco—MG

PENGUIN WORKSHOP
An imprint of Penguin Random House LLC, New York

First published in the United States of America by Penguin Workshop,
an imprint of Penguin Random House LLC, New York, 2023

Text copyright © 2023 by Ellen Labrecque
Illustrations copyright © 2023 by Penguin Random House LLC

Visit us online at penguinrandomhouse.com.

Library of Congress Cataloging-in-Publication Data is available.

Printed in the United States of America

ISBN 9780399544101 (paperback)   10 9 8 7 6 5 4 3 2 1 WOR
ISBN 9780399544125 (library binding)   10 9 8 7 6 5 4 3 2 1 WOR

Contents

Who Was Frank Sinatra?

On December 30, 1942, two days before the new year, a slender singer walked onto the stage of the Paramount Theatre in New York City. Over three thousand fans—mostly teenage girls— shrieked and screamed in excitement. Some cried tears of happiness.

"The sound that greeted me was absolutely deafening," the star said later. "It was a tremendous roar . . . I was scared stiff."

The singer's name was Frank Sinatra. He sang romantic songs in a soft and low voice. This style of singing is called crooning. And Frank was a crooner. But Frank didn't write his own music. In fact, many of the songs he sang had been written many years earlier. They were considered old standards. But when Frank sang, he put a new spin on them—holding some notes longer, while releasing others in short bursts.

Frank was also good looking and dressed nicely. He had bright blue eyes, white sparkly teeth, and curly thick brown hair. He was twenty-seven years old, but he could have been mistaken for someone much younger.

Frank began singing. He sang slow songs that were filled with emotion about love and heartbreak. His voice sounded as soft and warm as a fleece blanket. The girls were in love with Frank's songs. They thought they were in love with Frank, too!

When the show ended, teenagers in the crowd rushed to the backstage door. They wanted to be near Frank. They hoped to get his autograph. The crowd spilled out into the New York streets and caused traffic jams. The teens loved him because he had a voice that sounded like nothing they had ever heard before.

Before that night, Frank had been singing with a sixteen-piece orchestra as part of a big band. He had recently left to sing on his own. Frank didn't realize how popular he had become and how much his music would inspire fans for many years to follow.

CHAPTER 1
The Only Child

Francis Albert Sinatra was born on December 12, 1915, in Hoboken, New Jersey. His mother, Natalie "Dolly" Sinatra, was less than five feet tall and weighed just ninety pounds. But Frank, as he was called, weighed over thirteen pounds, which made the home birth difficult for Dolly.

"I just didn't want to come out," Frank jokingly said many years later when describing his birth.

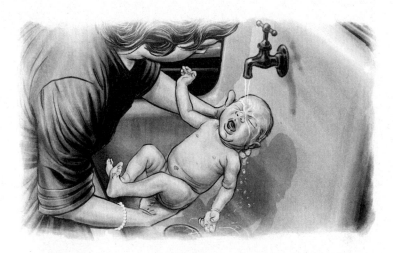

The doctor worked hard to help Dolly deliver the baby. But when baby Frank arrived, he wasn't breathing. Frank's grandmother grabbed her grandson and ran cold water over him. Frank gave a loud cry. He was alive!

The doctor successfully saved Frank and his mother, but the delivery accidently hurt Frank— especially one ear, a cheek, and his neck. Frank had scars for the rest of his life. The eardrum of the injured ear was punctured. (It had a hole in it.) Dolly was also injured; she could not have any more children.

Hoboken, New Jersey

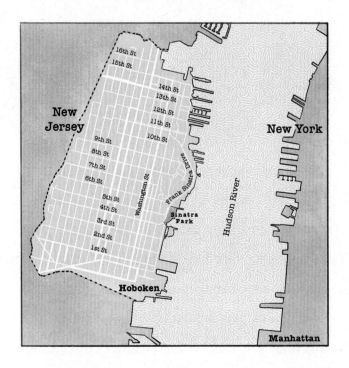

Hoboken, New Jersey, is a small city across the Hudson River from Manhattan, which is part of New York City. Hoboken's nickname is the mile-square city, but it actually covers close to two square miles. In the first half of the twentieth century, the city was filled with immigrants from all over the world. Most of the people didn't have much money. Many of them worked in the local factories or down at the dockyards, loading and unloading boats.

Today, many of the people living in Hoboken are wealthy and educated commuters who take a train or ferry into New York City every day for work. Hoboken is home to hundreds of fancy restaurants, bars, and luxury apartments. The city is still famous for two things: One of the first recorded baseball games was played there in 1846. And it is the hometown of Frank Sinatra. There are parks and streets all over Hoboken named in Frank's honor.

Frank lived with his mother and father, Martin Sinatra, in a cold-water apartment on Monroe Street. This meant that the apartment had a sink that ran only cold water. To take a hot shower, they had to use a bathroom shared with other families in the building.

Dolly was a tough, outspoken woman. She worked as a chocolate dipper in a local candy factory. She was also a midwife, someone who helps deliver babies. When she wasn't working, Dolly sang at weddings and family events and sometimes even at restaurants.

As loud as Dolly could be, Martin Sinatra was quiet and shy. He listened to what Dolly told him to do, and mostly he did it. Martin was a boxer when Frank was born. When Frank was older, his father became a firefighter.

Martin Sinatra

Dolly's and Martin's families both came to the United States from Italy. They were very proud of their Italian roots. Frank grew up to be a proud Italian American, too.

When Frank was a child in Hoboken, there were Italian, Irish, Jewish, German, and Black neighborhoods. Frank's family lived in the Italian neighborhood. Frank tried to get along with everybody. Sometimes, kids called one another mean names based on what race or religion they were. Not Frank. He didn't think race or religion mattered. He thought people were just people.

"Something rubbed me the wrong way," Frank said about the name-calling when he was older.

Frank did have a temper, though. Sometimes, kids called him Scarface because of the scars left from his difficult birth. Frank did not like that at all. Once after this happened, he marched to the home of the doctor who had delivered him.

He had planned to yell at him for causing the scars. Luckily, the doctor wasn't home at the time.

Frank's mother and father worked a lot, so Frank's grandparents often watched him. But when Frank's parents were around, they spoiled their son. Most families in Hoboken had a lot of kids. The Sinatras had only Frank. They bought him nice clothes and toys. Kids in his neighborhood called him Slacksey because he seemed to have a new pair of pants for every day of the week. He also was one of the few kids in his lower-income neighborhood who had his own bicycle.

"Being an only child made all the difference," said one of Frank's neighbors. "He didn't have to share with brothers and sisters. He even had his own bedroom. None of the rest of us had half of what he had."

In 1926, when Frank was eleven, his mother and father opened a bar. They called it Marty O'Brien's. They used an Irish name because Hoboken was filled with Irish immigrants. They thought they would get more customers that way. Frank spent a lot of time at the bar as a kid. The bar had a self-playing piano. Sometimes, Frank would stand on top of the piano and sing along with the tune, performing for the customers. Sometimes, he would receive tips for his singing, and that made Frank very happy.

CHAPTER 2
On the Rise

As Frank grew up, he continued to sing. He performed with his school and church choirs. When Frank wasn't singing, he listened to the radio. In the days before television, families tuned in to the radio to be entertained. He also went to see others perform live. Once, he heard a singer named Bing Crosby. Bing sang quietly. He let the microphone carry his voice around the room.

Frank had never heard a singer do this before.

Frank saw Bing Crosby as his first idol because he sang so easily. He thought Bing was so relaxed and casual. Frank loved to sing at his school's dances. What he didn't love, though, was actually going to school. As a teenager in A. J. Demarest High School in Hoboken, Frank didn't do his homework. He skipped school often. And when he was there, he sometimes got in trouble for pulling pranks. One time during an assembly, he released pigeons in the auditorium.

Bing Crosby (1903–1977)

Harry Lillis "Bing" Crosby was an American singer, actor, and comedian. The most famous song he ever sang was "White Christmas," the best-selling single of all time. It has sold more than fifty million copies all over the world.

Bing grew up in Spokane, Washington. His nickname came from his favorite comic strip,

The Bingville Bugle. Bing's family was musical. He started singing and playing the drums while in college at Gonzaga University in Spokane.

Bing sang like he was having a private conversation with one person. Many of his songs were slow, simple ones called ballads. He also starred in many popular films. He won the Academy Award for best actor in a leading role for the 1944 film *Going My Way.*

In 1931, when Frank was sixteen, he left school for good. Frank's father was disappointed in his son. Marty couldn't read or write himself, but he wanted his son to have a good education. He called his son a quitter. Frank explained that his dream was to be a professional singer, and he begged his dad to give him a chance to make that happen.

Frank began singing in clubs at night and on the weekends. He sang with small bands. He wasn't paid much to sing, so he also worked many jobs during the day. He delivered newspapers to people's houses. He also worked at the Hoboken dockyards, loading and unloading boats docked along the Hudson River.

In September 1935, not long before his twentieth birthday, Frank got his first big break. He auditioned for a national radio show called *Major Bowes and the Original Amateur Hour*. The best singers were selected to perform with other Major Bowes winners on a tour throughout the United States. Frank sang with three other singers from his hometown. They called themselves the Hoboken Four. Frank's group won first prize!

The Hoboken Four

"Frank stood out as the best in the group," said a former Major Bowes staff member. "After the show people would flock backstage. The others would be asked to sign an autograph or two, but Frank was practically torn apart."

CHAPTER 3
Going Solo

Over the next few years, Frank took singing lessons. He practiced hard to make sure his voice was as finely tuned as possible. It was naturally high-pitched, but he wanted to have range, so he learned how to sing the high notes *and* the low notes. Frank was determined to be the best singer in the world.

"He was a boy who never stopped studying," Frank's singing teacher said.

On February 4, 1939, Frank, age twenty-three, married Nancy Barbato. They had been dating since they'd met at the Jersey Shore five years earlier. They were married in a church in Nancy's hometown of Jersey City. The couple couldn't afford to go on a honeymoon. Instead, they used what money they had to rent an apartment in Jersey City. The rent was forty-two dollars a month.

Frank marries Nancy Barbato

The same year Frank and Nancy were married, Frank got a job as a singing waiter at the Rustic Cabin restaurant in Englewood Cliffs, New Jersey, not far from their home in Jersey City. Frank sang onstage and waited on tables between his performances. A radio station recorded Frank and other singers while they were onstage. Frank's mother and father were so proud to hear their son sing on the radio.

Many other people heard Frank sing, too. His voice stood out from others. Harry James was a trumpet player in a big band that toured around the United States. After hearing Frank's voice on the radio, he went to the Rustic Cabin to see him perform in person.

Harry James

Watching Frank live that night, Harry said, "I felt the hairs on the back of my neck rising. I knew he was destined to be a great vocalist."

Harry asked Frank to join him and his band as a singer to tour the country. Frank immediately said yes. He toured with Harry for a few months until a bigger opportunity came his way. The lead singer of an even more popular group—the Tommy Dorsey band—had quit.

Tommy Dorsey

The Tommy Dorsey band had big hits on the radio. It also performed in more places and in front of bigger audiences than Harry James's band did. In January 1940, Tommy asked Frank if he would join the band, and Frank jumped at the chance.

Tommy Dorsey was a famous trombone player. He could hold his breath for a long time. This meant he could play note after note, without taking a breath. Frank started to do the same thing with his singing. He sang like he was speaking a very long sentence that didn't have any punctuation. The audience couldn't wait to hear what he might sing next.

Over the next couple of months in 1940,
Frank became a star. At first, crowds came to see
the entire Dorsey band. But soon, it became clear
that the band was selling so many tickets because
the fans wanted to hear—and see—Frank.

Big Bands

Big bands were a popular type of jazz ensemble in the 1930s and 1940s. They were musical groups made up of ten or more musicians. Each band included different instrumental sections, such as trumpets, saxophones, trombones, and a rhythm section, which included drums. The bands also had vocalists, who sang while the musicians played.

The most important talent of any big band was its bandleader. The bandleader is like a conductor who may play an instrument, too. The bandleader arranges and creates material for the band to play. Many bandleaders, including Tommy Dorsey, became famous.

Big band music was played on the radio. The bands also toured and played in concert halls throughout the United States. But their popularity dipped when the lead singers became more famous

than the bands themselves. It became hard for
concert halls to pay so many musicians night after
night. By the mid-1950s, young fans also wanted to
listen to smaller bands and faster music like rock
and roll.

When Frank sang, his audience felt like he was looking at and singing to each of them. Teenage girls became Frank's biggest fans. Sometimes when he sang, they screamed in delight. In 1940, the band recorded one of its songs in a studio. It was called "I'll Never Smile Again," and it became the most popular song in the country that year.

Frank decided he didn't want to be part of a group anymore. He was ready to be a big star, like Bing Crosby. Frank's final performance with the band was on September 3, 1942. Tommy Dorsey and his band wished him well, and Frank left the stage to begin the next chapter of his career.

CHAPTER 4
Sinatra Mania

After Frank left the Tommy Dorsey band, he spent time with his family and rested. At the time, Frank and Nancy lived in Hasbrouck Heights, New Jersey, a small town near New York City. They had a daughter, also named Nancy, who was two years old.

After a couple of months, Frank got a phone call that would change his life. The manager of the Paramount Theatre in New York City asked Frank to perform solo on December 30, 1942. Frank agreed right away.

"This is the moment that is going to make me or break me," Frank thought at the time. "If I'm not good at the Paramount Theatre, I am dead."

When Frank walked onstage at the Paramount in December 1942, the crowd—mostly teenage girls—squealed in happiness.

"Frankeeeee! Frankeeeee!" they screamed.

Security guards tried to calm down the crowd, but doing so was impossible. "There is nothing you can do when you have three thousand people standing up and screaming at something," one guard said.

Because Frank was such a big hit, the Paramount booked him to perform every night for the next two months.

The Paramount Theatre (1926–1964)

The Paramount Theatre was a famous 3,664-seat venue that showed movies and also hosted live performances. It was located right in the middle of the Times Square district—a tourist destination in New York City illuminated by bright lights and bustling with activity from theaters and restaurants.

During the 1940s, the Paramount was the place to be for people who wanted to see live bands perform in the United States. In the 1950s and early 1960s, rock and roll bands such as the Beatles performed there.

The theater was closed in 1964. It was later turned into a restaurant and office space for the *New York Times* newspaper.

When Frank wasn't performing live, he sang for a CBS radio show called *Your Hit Parade*, which debuted in January 1943. His voice was broadcast into living rooms all over the United States.

Teenage girls, called bobby-soxers, formed Frank Sinatra fan clubs. These girls got their

name from the bobby socks they wore with their skirts. The socks were white and gathered around their ankles. Frank was soon nicknamed Swoonatra because the girls would swoon, or faint, when they heard him sing.

Frank thought the girls liked him so much because they missed their real boyfriends, who were off fighting in World War II. Frank could not fight because of the injuries he'd endured when he was born. He was classified by the United States Army as a 4F, which meant he was medically unfit to serve in the war.

After Frank finished his series of concerts at the Paramount Theatre, he sang in concert theaters all over the United States. Everywhere Frank went, large crowds of teenage girls followed. Long lines of fans circled around theaters before and after his shows, with girls waiting hours to try to get a glimpse of the star.

Fans even camped outside of Frank's house.

World War II (1939–1945)

World War II was fought between the Allies and the Axis powers. The Allies included democracies like the United States, Great Britain, France, and Canada, plus the communist Soviet Union. The Axis powers were led by Germany, Italy, and Japan. The leader of Germany, Adolf Hitler, believed white German people were the master race, and he wanted to dominate Europe. His Nazi organization killed, hurt, and tortured many other people, especially those who were Jewish. The Allies were trying to stop him.

The United States joined the Allies in 1941 when Japan bombed its naval base at Pearl Harbor, in Hawaii, about two years after the war in Europe had started. More than sixteen million Americans fought in World War II. This was about 11 percent of the country's total population at

Adolf Hitler with German children during World War II

the time. Over four hundred thousand Americans died in the war. But the Allies won the war in 1945.

"We tried asking them to go home, but they wouldn't leave," said Frank's wife, Nancy. "I'd feel so sorry for them I would send out doughnuts and something for them to drink."

Frank was a celebrity. And he was also quite rich. He earned a combined three million dollars in 1944 and 1945 through concert tickets, record sales, and radio performances. Frank couldn't believe how far he had come from his Hoboken days. And The Voice, as he was now called, was about to travel even farther.

Frank had become one of the world's most famous singers. Now he hoped to be a movie star, too. One of his first movies was a musical called *Higher and Higher*. He played a young man who also happened to be named Frank.

The film was released to good reviews in January 1944. That same month, Frank and Nancy had a second child, their son, Francis Wayne. By the end of that year, Frank moved his growing family from New Jersey to the San

Fernando Valley, in California. Known to locals as the Valley, it's close to Hollywood, the center of the movie business.

Hollywood

Since the 1900s, Hollywood, California, has been the home for movie studios and, more recently, the television industry. It is a famous neighborhood in Los Angeles, California. Actors and actresses have traveled there from all over the world to try to become stars and make their dreams come true.

Hollywood is a specific location. But when

people talk about Hollywood, they might also be referring to the entertainment industry in general. The city's year-round sunny weather is ideal for making movies, and successful film studios helped Los Angeles grow into a giant American city. Many famous movie and television stars live in the wealthy neighborhoods surrounding Hollywood.

One of Los Angeles's most famous landmarks is the Hollywood sign that is set high above the city.

The Sinatras' new house in the Valley was a beautiful mansion. It was right next to a lake where the family could swim and fish. Frank and Nancy became friends with other famous actors and singers who lived nearby. They threw giant parties where up to two hundred people might come to relax, laugh, and have fun.

In 1945, Frank costarred in the movie *Anchors Aweigh* with dancer Gene Kelly. Before the movie started filming, Gene offered Frank some advice. He told Frank that to really be a

movie star, he couldn't just stand there and sing. He had to learn how to dance, too. So Frank responded to Gene by saying, "Great, when do we start?" Frank learned everything he could from Gene.

Frank with Gene Kelly

Gene Kelly (1912–1996)

Eugene Curran Kelly was born on August 23, 1912, in Pittsburgh, Pennsylvania. He studied ballet

and other styles of dance. As an adult, Gene, as he came to be known, ran a dance studio with his family in Pittsburgh. In 1938, he moved to New York City, determined to dance and sing in Broadway musicals. He later moved to Hollywood to become a movie star.

Gene made his most famous movie, *Singin' in the Rain*, in 1952. In one scene, Gene dances with an umbrella and swings on a lamppost while singing, of course, in the rain.

Once filming began, Frank looked like he had danced his whole life. *Anchors Aweigh* was a huge hit and won an Academy Award that year.

That same year, Frank also starred as himself in a short film titled *The House I Live In*. It tried to teach kids that all people are equal, no matter their race or religion. Frank truly believed in this message. It was something he learned as a boy in Hoboken and never forgot.

Frank stars in *The House I Live In*

The Academy Awards

The Academy Awards ceremony is held every year in Los Angeles, California, to honor people who work in the film industry. The awards, which were first handed out in 1929, are given by the Academy of Motion Picture Arts and Sciences for excellence in acting, directing, screenwriting, and other categories. The winner of each category is given a bronze statue coated in 24-karat gold. The statue is of a knight holding a sword and standing on a film reel. It is called an Oscar and got its nickname when a librarian for the Academy said the statue looked like her uncle Oscar.

Frank had become the biggest star in the world—he was in movies, on the radio, and he still did live performances throughout the United States. He released a new single almost every month. Frank's busy career kept him on the road and away from his family most of the time. He and Nancy now had three children. Their second daughter, Christina, had been born on Father's Day in June 1948.

Separated from his family when he worked, Frank began to date other women. He especially liked to date other movie stars. Frank was photographed with a beautiful actress named Ava Gardner in 1949. Their pictures were printed in newspapers and magazines all over the United States. This upset

Ava Gardner

Nancy. She didn't want to see her husband with other women. He was married to her. But Frank had fallen in love with Ava. Finally, Nancy could not take it anymore. Nancy and Frank were divorced on October 31, 1951. A week later, Frank married Ava.

With all this change in Frank's personal life, his professional life was changing, too—and not for the better. Frank's next few movies weren't very successful. His records were not selling, either. The new generation of teenagers liked faster, more upbeat songs. They didn't want to listen to Frank's slow ballads anymore. They also were disappointed in Frank. His fans imagined him as a good father and husband. They didn't like seeing him with his new wife.

In 1952, Frank was only thirty-seven years old. But suddenly, it seemed as if no one was interested in him anymore.

Frank and Ava Gardner's wedding

CHAPTER 6
He's Back!

Frank needed a lucky break to turn his career around. It came in the form of the 1953 movie *From Here to Eternity*. The film was based on a best-selling book about World War II.

Even though Frank's career was not going well, his wife, Ava Gardner, was still a big star. This meant important people in the business would listen to her advice. Ava asked the head of the movie studio to cast Frank in the part of Angelo Maggio in *From Here to Eternity*. Maggio was an Italian American who was down on his luck. It seemed like the perfect part for her husband. Another actor was supposed to play Maggio, but that actor wanted a lot of money.

Frank was willing to work for far less. He wanted the part so badly, he would have probably done the movie for free. The studio decided to give Frank a chance.

Frank worked harder than he ever had before. He showed up early and worked until late. When he stepped on the set, Frank became Angelo Maggio.

From Here to Eternity was a smash hit from the day it was released. It earned more money than any other film in 1953 and was one of the top-earning films of the decade. Critics also enjoyed

Drive-in screening of *From Here to Eternity*

Frank's performance. Maggio was his first serious role without a singing part. He had made it seem like he wasn't acting at all.

On March 25, 1954, Frank won the Academy Award for best supporting actor. Frank was so excited, he jogged down the aisle to receive the award.

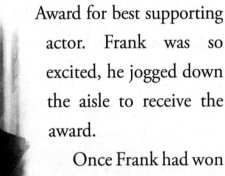

Once Frank had won his Academy Award, people suddenly wanted to hear him sing again, too. He had released the song "I've Got the World on a String" in 1953. But now it suddenly became popular. The ballad had been written over twenty years earlier, but Frank sang it in a whole new way. When he sang the line "I've got the world on a string, sittin' on a rainbow," he sang like a man who had been through hard times but had survived to tell his story.

At thirty-nine, Frank was no longer a young boy but a mature man. He had some wrinkles on his face and he liked to wear a type of hat called a fedora, to hide that he was losing some of his hair. His voice had grown deeper and was more soulful.

His audience had changed right along with him. He was no longer the idol of teenage girls. Instead, Frank's biggest fans were now parents, appreciating him just as he was.

In 1955, Frank appeared on the cover of *TIME* magazine. In the article, the writer said that Frank "was well away on a second career that promises to be if anything more brilliant than the first."

More successful albums and movies followed.

A movie scene from *High Society*
with Frank Sinatra and Bing Crosby

In 1956, Frank starred in another romantic comedy, *High Society*. Frank's costar was his boyhood idol, Bing Crosby. Frank, though, had become an even bigger star than Bing! The movie earned a lot of money.

In 1959, Frank released the album *Come Dance with Me!* In 1960, it won the Grammy Award as album of the year—the top prize in American music.

Frank had some low points in his career. But now, he was back on top.

CHAPTER 7
The Rat Pack

As Frank's popularity continued to rise, he began spending a lot of his time in Las Vegas, Nevada. In the 1950s, Las Vegas was a shiny new city in the Mojave Desert. Casinos and big hotels had been built there after World War II. People came by the millions to gamble and to see big shows. Frank was one of the hottest attractions in town. He performed at a hotel and casino called the Sands. People packed into the concert hall to see Frank sing.

When Frank wasn't performing, he was often seen hanging around the casinos with a group of friends who were also singers and actors. They called themselves the Rat Pack.

Frank was the leader of the Rat Pack. One of the other members was a Black singer named

Sammy Davis Jr. In the 1950s, Black people were often treated worse than white people because of the color of their skin. White and Black people had to sleep in separate hotels and eat at different restaurants.

Sammy Davis Jr.

They attended separate schools and churches. The facilities for Black people were never as nice as those for white people. Frank, though, was committed to civil rights for all people. And because of this, Frank insisted Sammy be allowed to stay in the same hotels and perform in the same venues as the other members of the Rat Pack. And because he was Frank Sinatra, many businesses and hotels listened to him and made exceptions for Sammy.

The Rat Pack

The Rat Pack was a group of entertainers who hung out together in the 1950s and 1960s. The group included Frank Sinatra, Dean Martin, Sammy Davis Jr., Peter Lawford, and Joey Bishop. They were seen together around Las Vegas going to parties and the casinos. They always looked like they were having fun.

The Rat Pack performed together onstage and in movies—their most famous one being *Ocean's Eleven* in 1960. The movie was so popular, it was remade in 2001 starring actors George Clooney and Brad Pitt.

Frank Sinatra, Dean Martin, Sammy Davis Jr.,
Peter Lawford, and Joey Bishop

FRANK SINATRA 🎤🎤 DEAN MARTIN
SAMMY DAVIS ᴊʀ. PETER LAWFORD
ANGIE DICKINSON.

"OCEAN'S 11"

Frank and the rest of the Rat Pack worked hard in Las Vegas. They performed many shows and sang constantly. They also starred in movies like *Ocean's Eleven*. Frank played Danny Ocean. He was the leader of a group that decides to steal money from several Las Vegas casinos.

Although Frank wasn't robbing casinos in real life, he was spending most of his free time in them. Frank and Ava had divorced in 1957, and he continued to hang out with the Rat Pack and his Hollywood friends. It seemed like Frank never needed to sleep.

"We would do two shows a night, get to bed at four-thirty or five a.m., get up at seven or eight,

FRANK S
DEAN M
SAMMY
PETER L
JOEY B

and go to work on a movie," said Peter Lawford. "We'd come back and do it all over again."

During a four-week period in 1960, thirty-four thousand people came to see the Rat Pack's show at the Sands; called the Summit, it was a combination of singing, dancing, and telling jokes. The show was so popular, guests offered to pay one hundred dollars for a ticket that originally sold for three dollars. Frank, of course, was the star of it all.

CHAPTER 8
Star Power

Frank was always very interested in politics, and when he became famous, there were many politicians who wanted to meet him. He was even invited to the White House, the home of the president of the United States, many times. Frank became a big supporter of Senator John Fitzgerald Kennedy of Massachusetts. Frank had met Senator Kennedy, who was nicknamed JFK for his initials, through his friend Peter Lawford, the senator's brother-in-law. Frank especially liked JFK because of his views on civil rights. And Senator Kennedy enjoyed the Hollywood lifestyle that Frank led. They were a perfect combination of celebrity and political status.

In 1960, JFK was running to become the president of the United States. Frank was one of the biggest stars in the world. If Frank said he was supporting Kennedy, other people, especially Italian Americans, would want to support him, too. Frank did more than just talk. He also raised a lot of money for Senator Kennedy through performances and concerts.

Frank talking with John Fitzgerald Kennedy

On November 8, 1960, JFK beat Richard
Nixon in a very close race. Many people thought
Frank Sinatra's support played a big part in the
victory.

John Fitzgerald Kennedy (1917–1963)

John Fitzgerald Kennedy was born on May 29, 1917, in Brookline, Massachusetts. He was the second of nine children. John's family was very wealthy. His father loved politics and served as the US ambassador to Great Britain.

John graduated from Harvard University in 1940. He joined the United States Navy during World War II and was awarded a medal for bravery.

At age forty-three, he became the thirty-fifth president of the United States. He was the youngest president ever elected when he defeated Richard M. Nixon in November 1960. Before becoming president, John, a member of the Democratic party, was a senator for Massachusetts.

John was a very popular president. With his beautiful wife, Jackie—and their children, Caroline and John Jr.—he represented a new and younger generation of leadership. Before he could run for reelection, a former marine named Lee Harvey Oswald shot and killed him in Dallas, Texas, in 1963.

"I know we are all indebted to a great friend, Frank Sinatra," President Kennedy said at the inaugural gala to celebrate his presidential win.

Frank's daughter, Nancy—who was at that time a grown woman with a singing career of her

Nancy Sinatra,
Frank's daughter

own—was also there that night. "Dad had risen from the streets of Hoboken to become the biggest and most powerful star in show business," Nancy said. "It was a moment to savor for a lifetime."

CHAPTER 9
Going Out on Top

Frank continued to sing and act over the next decade. After twenty years in entertainment, he had learned how to be a smart businessman.

By 1965, Frank owned two movie companies as well as his own recording company. He also ran an airplane charter business. He personally employed around seventy-five people, including secretaries who answered his fan mail and bodyguards who protected him everywhere he went. It was estimated that Frank by then earned about three and half million dollars per year. In addition to being nicknamed The Voice, Frank was now called The Chairman of the Board. This meant he was the boss, the one in charge of everything.

In 1966, in Las Vegas, Frank married a young actress named Mia Farrow. Frank was fifty years old, and Mia was just twenty-one. They had met on a movie set. Frank expected his wife to take care of him and their home, but Mia was busy with her own career. Often, they didn't see each other for weeks because they were both acting in different movies all around

Frank and Mia Farrow

the world. Their marriage lasted less than three years.

In 1969, Frank released his forty-ninth album. It was titled *My Way*, which was also the title of the lead single from the album. It became one of Frank's most well-known songs.

"My Way"

"My Way" was written for Frank Sinatra by songwriter Paul Anka. Paul adapted the tune from a French song called "Comme d'habitude," which means "as usual."

The song was about living your life the way you want, and never apologizing for doing so. Many other performers, including Elvis Presley, sang "My Way," but Frank's version was the most famous. The song was as popular in the United Kingdom as it was in the United States. It spent seventy-five weeks on the UK's Top Forty songs list—a record that lasted until 2020.

Even though "My Way" was one of Frank's most famous songs, he thought it made him sound boastful.

"I know it's a very big hit—and I love having big hits," Frank said. "But I hate immodesty, and that's how I feel every time I sing the song."

Frank may have lived "his way" for many years, but he was getting tired. All the performances,

the traveling, and the late-night parties had finally worn him down. In 1971, when Frank was fifty-five years old, he announced he was retiring. He decided to say goodbye to his fans the way he knew best. He chose to perform eleven of his most famous songs in a concert on June 13 that year at the Ahmanson Theatre in Los Angeles. Over five thousand people were in the audience, including the vice president of the United States, Spiro Agnew; the governor of California and future US president, Ronald Reagan; and movie stars including Cary Grant and Jimmy Stewart.

Frank started his set with "All or Nothing at All" and finished with "My Way." The crowd called for Frank to continue singing, and he did. He ended with the song "Angel Eyes." The last line of that song is, "Excuse me while I disappear." Then the stage went dark. Frank was gone.

CHAPTER 10
Still Got It

At first, Frank told everyone his career was truly finished. He had made fifty-eight films and recorded two thousand songs across one hundred albums.

"I don't want to perform anymore," Frank had said earlier. "I'm not going to stop living. Maybe I am going to *start* living." He meant that maybe he could now begin to enjoy his personal life as much as he had his professional one.

Frank had always liked to paint, and he spent more time creating abstract art. He also took photographs and played golf. Whenever and wherever he traveled, Frank continued to be honored. The city of Palm Springs, California, held a Frank Sinatra Day and changed the name

of a road he lived on to Frank Sinatra Drive. In 1979, the city of Hoboken also renamed the Sinatras' riverfront road Frank Sinatra Drive.

Frank, though, soon grew restless in retirement. He had been working and traveling his entire adult life. He liked to be busy. He also liked to be the center of attention. He missed having the spotlight on him.

In November 1973, about a year and a half after his retirement concert, Frank appeared in a television special called *Frank Sinatra: Ol' Blue Eyes Is Back*. Ol' Blue Eyes had become one of his nicknames over the years. Frank had recently released an album under that same name. He sang many of his classic songs. Gene Kelly, his costar years before in *Anchors Aweigh*, was a guest star. The show was a hit. An estimated forty million people watched it.

In October 1974, Frank performed a live televised concert at Madison Square Garden in New York City.

The Garden is an indoor arena used for professional ice hockey and basketball games, boxing matches, and concerts. It can fit about twenty thousand people. Frank wanted to show everybody he was still the champion. The show was called *Frank Sinatra: The Main Event* and was packed with people. Millions more watched from home.

"It's like a champ returning to defend his title," wrote one newspaper reporter about Frank's performance. "When Sinatra came out of retirement, he came out swinging."

Frank—almost fifty-nine years old at the time—was no longer the skinny, curly haired young man that the bobby-soxers once screamed for. His face was more round than lean, and he wore a hairpiece to cover his baldness. But he still looked elegant in a perfectly pressed tuxedo. And his voice was still magical.

"The style is still all there," said one fan,

"and what's left of the voice still gets to me like no other voice, and it always will."

Barbara Marx and Frank

As Frank's career began to take off again, he also married for the fourth and final time. Frank wed Barbara Marx on July 11, 1976. Barbara had been a model and dancer, and the two of them had met years earlier but really connected in Las Vegas, where they were both performing. Unlike Mia Farrow, Barbara didn't want her own career anymore. She was happy to support Frank and his work.

By 1979, Frank was going to be sixty-four years old. He had been a professional singer for more than forty years. But he was finally about to sing the song he would be most remembered for. The song was called "New York, New York."

Throughout the 1980s, Frank performed at concerts around the world. Instead of slowing down as he got older, Frank sped up. He performed in front of bigger and bigger crowds. In 1980, he sang at a soccer stadium in Rio de Janeiro, Brazil, for 175,000 people. It was one of the largest concert crowds ever. In 1985, Frank was awarded the Presidential Medal of Freedom by President Ronald Reagan. It is the highest civilian honor in the United States.

He is "one of our most remarkable and distinguished Americans," President Reagan said about Frank.

"New York, New York"

"New York, New York" was written as the theme song for a 1977 movie with the same name. Singer and actress Liza Minnelli was the first performer to sing it.

Frank Sinatra first sang the song at a 1978 concert at Radio City Music Hall in New York City. He then recorded it for an album in 1979. Frank's version became an instant hit. The song begins:

Start spreading the news,

I'm leaving today

I want to be a part of it:

New York, New York

And the last lines are:

And if I can make it there,

I'm gonna make it anywhere

It's up to you

New York, New York

"New York, New York" is now played all over the city at big and small events. Most famously, it is played at the end of every New York Yankees home game. It is also played every year at the Times Square New Year's Day celebration.

Frank sang the song to end every one of his concerts after 1979. It was the last song he performed in public. He joined in with others and sang it at his eightieth birthday celebration that aired on television on December 14, 1995.

Frank receives the Presidential Medal of Freedom

Frank had become a beloved legend. Fans who bought tickets wanted to see him sing. But they also wanted to be able to tell their kids and grandkids: "I saw Frank Sinatra in concert!"

Frank with U2 singer, Bono

In 1993, Frank, then almost seventy-eight years old, recorded a new album for the first time in ten years. It was called *Duets* and included Frank singing his most famous songs with a new generation of music stars, such as Bono, the lead singer of the Irish band U2. The album sold millions of copies. In a review, one music critic wrote: "Is Sinatra half the singer he was in 1942 or 1956? Actually he's about three-fifths the singer he was—but that still makes him about twice the singer anyone else is."

CHAPTER 11
His Way

In 1994, Frank received a Legend award at the annual Grammys ceremony. But Frank still wasn't finished. He continued to perform through the next year. On February 25, 1995, however, Frank gave his final performance. It was for about twelve hundred people who attended a private celebrity golf tournament in Las Vegas. During the previous year, Frank hadn't been as sharp as he used to be. He sometimes forgot words to the songs he had been singing for over fifty years. But on the night of his last performance, Frank sang like a man twenty years younger. At the end of the show, when the applause from the audience finally died down, Frank asked with sadness: "You mean it's time to go home?"

In December 1995, Frank Sinatra turned eighty years old. Newspapers around the world celebrated his birthday. A New York radio station played nothing but Frank Sinatra albums for a week straight. A live television special called *Sinatra: 80 Years My Way* aired on December 14. Frank was in the audience with his wife, Barbara. Famous music stars—including another musician, Bruce Springsteen, who was also born in New Jersey—each performed one classic Sinatra song.

Bruce Springsteen (1949–)

Bruce Springsteen was born in Freehold, New Jersey, on September 23, 1949. He got his first guitar when he was a teenager and never stopped playing.

Bruce, who is nicknamed The Boss, writes songs about working-class people trying to make their way in the world. He plays with the E Street band.

Unlike Frank, Bruce writes a lot of his own songs. He released his top-grossing album, *Born in the USA*, in 1984. It has sold thirty million copies around the world and includes seven hit singles. To date, Bruce has sold over 150 million records worldwide.

The Boss said he first heard Frank Sinatra's voice as a kid when one of Frank's songs was played on a jukebox. Bruce's mom asked her son to stop and listen.

"That's Frank Sinatra," Bruce's mom said. "He's from New Jersey too."

At the end of the show, Frank joined all the singers onstage and sang the last few lines of "New York, New York."

The next few years of Frank's life were quiet. He was sick a lot and in and out of the hospital. Several of Frank's best friends—Dean Martin and Sammy Davis Jr., as well as his second wife, Ava Gardner—died.

"With each passing, I think my father loses a tiny piece of his spirit," said Frank's daughter Tina.

Although Frank wasn't around much when his kids were growing up, he developed good relationships with them later in his life. He was also close to his three grandchildren.

Frank with his children and granddaughters

Frank died of a heart attack on May 14, 1998. He was eighty-two years old. After news of his death was announced, the Empire State Building in New York City was lit up in blue in honor of Ol' Blue Eyes. The lights on the main street in Las Vegas, also called the Strip, were dimmed. People packed into churches in Hoboken, Frank's hometown, to say their goodbyes.

When Frank was younger, a reporter asked how he wanted to be remembered. "I would like to be remembered as a man who brought innovation to popular singing," Frank said. "I would like to be remembered as a man who had a wonderful time living his life, and who had good friends, and a fine family. I think that would be it."

More than four hundred family members and friends and attended Frank's funeral, held on May 20, 1998, in Beverly Hills, California. Crowds of fans lined the streets outside the church service. At the end of the service, a recording of Frank singing "Put Your Dreams Away" was played. Frank's son, Frank Jr., spoke about his dad at the funeral.

"He sang for the world for sixty years," Frank Jr., said. "Today, and last night, everyone sang for him, and he listened." Frank was buried at a cemetery near his mother and father, who had both died years earlier.

Frank's music is still reaching millions of people. In the 2016 animated movie *Sing*, a mouse belts out "My Way." In restaurants, airports, sports venues, and many other public places, Frank's songs can often be heard blaring from a loudspeaker.

During his long life, Frank sang in over five thousand concerts, appeared on over nine hundred radio and television shows, and acted in sixty films. He is remembered as one of the greatest singers of the twentieth century, if not the greatest of all time. And as long as music exists, Frank Sinatra will live on forever.

Timeline of Frank Sinatra's Life

1915 — Francis Albert Sinatra is born on December 12 in Hoboken, New Jersey

1935 — Appears on *Major Bowes and the Original Amateur Hour*, a national radio show, on September 8

1939 — Marries Nancy Barbato on February 4

1940 — Becomes lead singer of the Tommy Dorsey band

1942 — Performs at the Paramount Theatre on December 30

1951 — Marries Ava Gardner on November 7

1954 — Wins the Academy Award for best supporting actor on March 25

1960 — Performs with the Rat Pack at the Sands hotel and casino in Las Vegas

1966 — Marries Mia Farrow on July 19

1969 — Releases "My Way," his forty-ninth album

1971 — Retires for the first time

1973 — Comes out of retirement to star in a television special on November 18

1976 — Marries Barbara Marx on July 11

1978 — Sings "New York, New York" for the first time at Radio City Music Hall in New York City

1995 — Gives his final performance on February 25

1998 — Dies on May 14

Timeline of the World

1914 — World War I begins in Europe

1935 — Musician Elvis Presley is born on January 8

1942 — Bing Crosby records the song "White Christmas" on May 29

1963 — United States president John F. Kennedy is assassinated on November 22

1968 — Civil rights leader Martin Luther King Jr. is assassinated on April 4

1969 — Neil Armstrong becomes the first man to set foot on the moon, on July 20

1970 — World celebrates first Earth Day on April 22

1981 — Lady Diana Spencer becomes the Princess of Wales when she marries Prince Charles on July 29

1986 — Dire Straits' album *Brothers in Arms* becomes the first CD to sell a million copies worldwide

1989 — The Berlin Wall that divided West and East Germany is taken down

1990 — Nelson Mandela, leader of the movement to end apartheid in South Africa, is freed on February 11 after twenty-seven years in prison

1998 — *Titanic* becomes the first film ever to earn more than a billion dollars in ticket sales worldwide

Bibliography

Freedland, Michael. *All the Way: A Biography of Frank Sinatra 1915–1998*. New York: St. Martin's Press, 1997.

Kaplan, James. *Frank: The Voice*. New York: Doubleday, 2010.

Kaplan, James. *Sinatra: The Chairman*. New York: Doubleday, 2015.

Sinatra, Nancy. *Frank Sinatra: My Father*. New York: Doubleday, 1985.

Sullivan, Robert, ed. *Life: Remembering Sinatra: 10 Years Later*. New York: TI Inc Books, 2008.

Summers, Anthony, and Robbyn Swan. *Sinatra: The Life*. New York: Alfred A. Knopf, 2005.

Taraborrelli, J. Randy. *Sinatra: Behind the Legend*. Secaucus, NJ: Rose Books, Inc., 1997.

Vanity Fair Icons. *Frank Sinatra: The Man, the Music, the Mystique*. New York: Conde Nast, 2018.

Website

www.sinatra.com